What's Inside Me?
My Brain

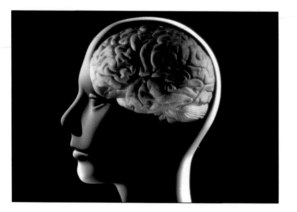

Dana Meachen Rau

MARSHALL CAVENDISH
NEW YORK

My Brain

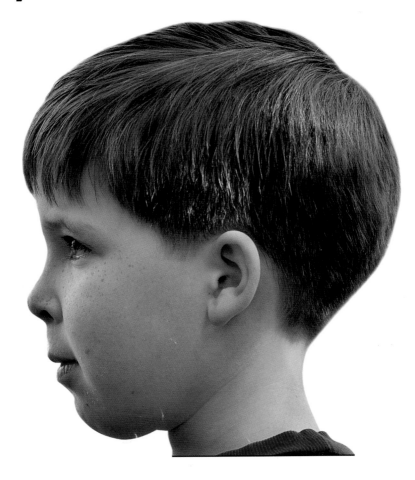

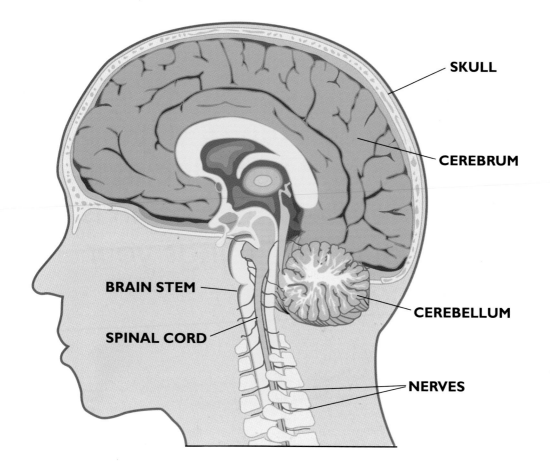

SKULL

CEREBRUM

BRAIN STEM

CEREBELLUM

SPINAL CORD

NERVES

3

Your body can run and jump.
It can see and hear. It can think
and *remember*. Your brain is in
charge of all the things your
body does.

Your brain looks like a big wrinkly lump of gray jelly. The hard bones of your *skull* protect your brain inside your head.

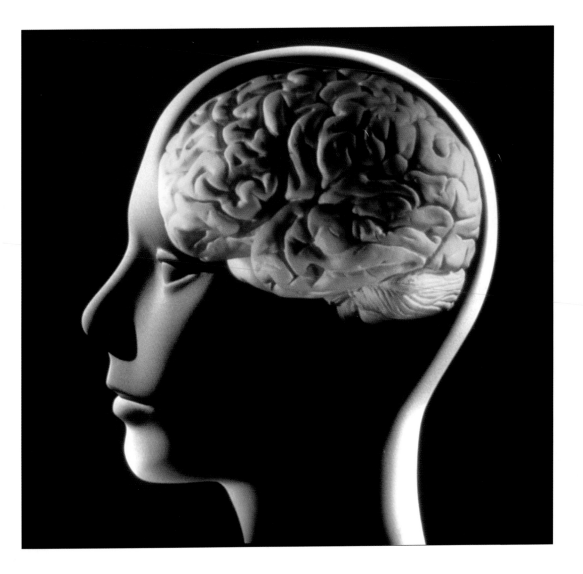

Your brain keeps your body alive. It makes your heart pump blood and your lungs breathe in air.

Your brain also controls when
you *swallow*.

10

Do you like to climb? Your brain tells your arms and legs how to move.

Your brain uses your senses to find out about the world around you. Your senses are hearing, smelling, tasting, touching, and seeing.

Look at this sign. It is red and has four letters. Your brain tells you it is a stop sign.

Did you learn how to solve a
new math problem at school?
Your brain is always *learning*.
It remembers things you may
need to know again.

Should you take the stairs or the elevator? Your brain helps you make choices.

Your brain is also in charge of feelings. Do you love to play the piano? Do scary movies make you worry? Everyone's brain is different. So everyone has different feelings.

Your brain is made of three parts. The *cerebrum* is in charge of thinking. The *cerebellum* is in charge of how your body moves. The *brain stem* is in charge of keeping your body alive.

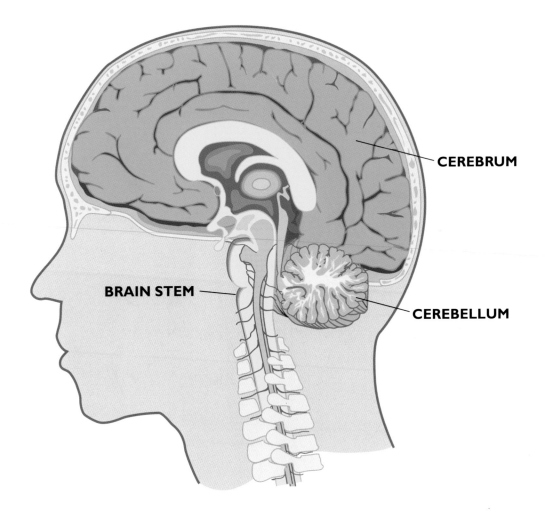

CEREBRUM

BRAIN STEM

CEREBELLUM

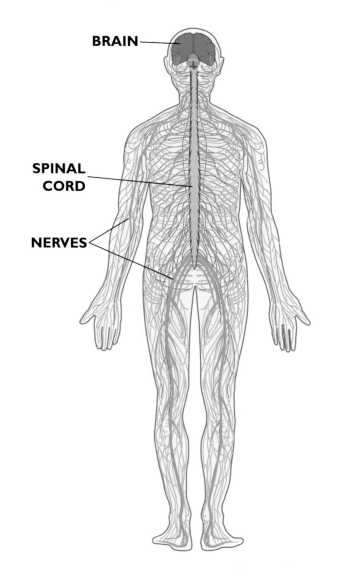

BRAIN

SPINAL CORD

NERVES

Your brain is connected to a *spinal cord*. The spinal cord runs down your back.

Nerves branch off the spinal cord and run to every part of your body. They are like wires.

Your brain uses nerves
to send messages to parts
of your body. Nerves
send messages back to
the brain, too.

Your nerves at work

Have you ever touched something hot? Your hurt finger sends a message along the nerves to the spinal cord and up to the brain. *"Ouch!"*

Then your brain sends a message back to your finger. *"Do not touch!"*

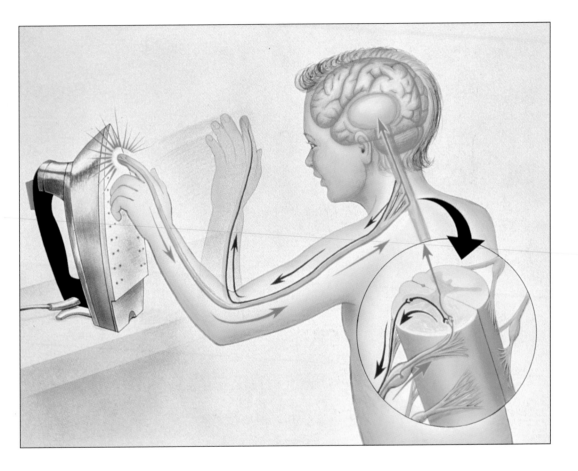

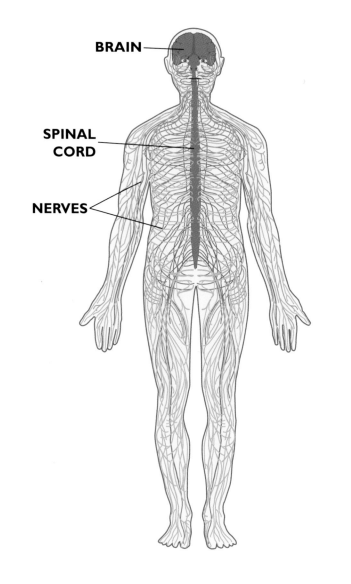

BRAIN

SPINAL CORD

NERVES

Your brain, spinal cord, and all the nerves in your body are called your *nervous system*.

Your brain works hard all day. At night, your brain makes you dream. While you sleep, your brain is getting ready for another busy day tomorrow!

Challenge Words

brain stem—The part of your brain in charge of running your inside parts.

cerebellum (ser-uh-BEH-luhm)—The part of your brain in charge of movement.

cerebrum (suh-REE-bruhm)—The part of your brain in charge of thinking.

learning—To gather new information.

nerves—Wire-like cords that run to all parts of your body.

nervous system—Your brain, spinal cord, and nerves.

remember—To think about something again.

skull—The bones in your head that protect your brain.

spinal cord (SPY-nuhl cord)—Part of the nervous system that runs down your back.

swallow—To move food from your tongue to your stomach.

Index

Page numbers in **boldface** are illustrations.

With thanks to Nanci Vargus, Ed.D. and Beth Walker Gambro, reading consultants

Benchmark Books
Marshall Cavendish
99 White Plains Road
Tarrytown, New York 10591-9001
www.marshallcavendish.com

Library of Congress Cataloging-in-Publication Data

Rau, Dana Meachen, 1971–
My brain / by Dana Meachen Rau.
p. cm. — (Bookworms: What's inside me?)
Includes index.
ISBN 0-7614-1781-8
1. Nervous system—Juvenile literature. I. Title. II. Series.

QP361.5.R38 2004
611'.8—dc22
2004002516

Photo Research by Anne Burns Images

/5,⌐

Cover Photo by *Corbis*/Christoph Wilhelm

The photographs in this book are used with the permission and through the courtesy of:
Corbis: pp. 5, 10, 15 Royalty Free; p. 8 Tom Stewart; p. 13 Alan Schein; p. 14 Charles Gupton; p. 17 Tom & Dee Ann McCarthy; p. 29 Kelly/Mooney Photography. *Jay Mallin*: p. 2. *Peter Arnold*: pp. 1, 7, 23 John Allison; p. 25 Alex Grey. *Visuals Unlimited*: p. 9 Pegasus.

Series design by Becky Terhune
Illustrations by Ian Warpole

Printed in China
1 3 5 6 4 2